In Conversation Vol. 4

"The world needs different kinds of minds

to work together."

~ **Temple Grandin,**

Also by T K Torme and Rachel Taylor

In Conversation Volume I   Silver Bow Publishing

In Conversation Volume II   Silver Bow Publishing

In Conversation Volume IIII   Silver Bow Publishing

And by T K Torme

Bull ... Silver Bow Publishing

Ite Missa Esst Vol I ... Silver Bow Publishing

Ite Missa Est Vol II ... Silver Bow Publishing

IN CONVERSATION
Volume IV

T K Torme

&

Rachel Taylor

720 Sixth Street, Unit #5
New Westminster, BC
V3L 3C5
CANADA

Title: In Conversation Volume IV
Authors: T K Torme and Rachel Taylor
Publisher: Silver Bow Publishing
Cover Art: "The Poetry Reading" painting by Candice James
Cover Layout and Design: Candice James
Editing: Candice James

All rights reserved including the right to reproduce or translate this book or any portions thereof, in any form without the permission of the publisher. Except for the use of short passages for review purposes, no part of this book may be reproduced, in part or in whole, or transmitted in any form or by any means, either by means electronically or mechanically, including photocopying, recording, or any information or storage retrieval system without prior permission in writing from the publisher or a licence from the Canadian Copyright Collective Agency (Access Copyright).

www.silverbowpublishing.com
info@silverbowpublishing.com
ISBN: 9781774031414- paperback
ISBN: 9781774031421- electronic book
© Silver Bow Publishing 2023

Library and Archives Canada Cataloguing in Publication

Title: In conversation. Volume IV / T.K. Torme & Rachel Taylor.
Other titles: In conversation (2020). Volume IV
Names: Torme, T. K., 1977- author. | Taylor, Rachel, 1987- author.
Identifiers: Canadiana (print) 20230202365 | Canadiana (ebook) 20230202403 | ISBN 9781774031414
   (softcover) | ISBN 9781774031421 (Kindle)
Subjects: LCSH: Haiku, Canadian—21st century. | CSH: Haiku, Canadian (English) | CSH: Canadian
   poetry (English)—21st century.
      Classification: LCC PS8285.H3 I54 2023 | DDC
         C811/.0410608—dc23

T K Torme Dedication

To Rachel Taylor whose awesome daily responses to my haiku poems without which my book would not have existed in this format.

To Candice James whose editing of my book made the words shine.

To Isabella Mori & Margo Lamont who have been super supportive of my writing.

To Malcom Van Delst & to all the Vancouver Grind Writers who have been so supportive of my writing since 2014.

To St. Scholastica my patron saint who has helped me write my haiku poems.

St. Scholastica, watch over me.

In Conversation Vol. 4

FOREWORD

The following haiku style poems in this book have 2 poems on each page representing a conversation between two people – T K Torme and Rachel Taylor.

The first poem on each page is by T K Torme

The second poem on each page is by Rachel Taylor.

In Conversation Vol. 4

In elevators,

I love to push all buttons

It is so much fun

It is so much fun

I love to push the buttons

Until we're fighting

What a sunny day

Perfect for St. Lucia

All bright crisp and clear

What a sunny day

Too bad to be stuck inside

For food therapy

Here's something for you:

I would really like to spend

New Year's Eve with you.

I would really like

To spend New Year's Eve in bed

Hiding from fireworks

The sun shines brightly

Dances all around the ground

Into my dark soul

Into my dark soul

A ray of light shines brightly

Only a pale flame

You don't get to say

Who is the right man for me

That is my own choice

You don't get to say

Whether or not my love is

Real and right and true

Happy one moment

Then crying outright the next

Calm neutral again

Trying to sort out

How to move through the next year

Happy one moment

On the outside world

I smile at other people

While I cry inside

On the outside, my

Temperament is sunny, but

Inside I'm angry

You don't have the right

To scare me with your death talk

Because that is cruel

Is such cruelty the

Legacy you wish to leave?

There's another way

I will not let you

Take away my only friend

Who's been good to me.

My only friend, who

Beams up at me everyday

What a good puppy

Your calling me names

It's really not that normal

Really quite twisted

Twisted up inside

Hearing your disdain, outrage

I know I'm no good

Eagles in the sky

Look how they soar in the air

Free from their burdens.

Miss serenity

Eagles soaring, hummingbirds

Free from gravity

What is wrong with me?

How do others find their spouse

While I'm all alone?

I feel all alone

Even surrounded by loud

And loving people

Is there something wrong

With me because I am still

Single, not married

Is there something wrong

With society? Worthy

Single or married

My elephant's grudge:

You left me when I was three

The last ghost to kill.

Forgive don't forget

Easy said but harder done

How can I let go?

Perhaps people can

Smell the abandonment that

Keeps others away

Keep others away

New people are dangerous

Anxiety says

Why do I feel so

Very horrible round you

You make me feel small

Insignificant

Was not anticipated

As my descriptor

I enjoy swimming

In the summer time when it

Is nice, sunny, warm

In the summertime

I try to build my dark walls

All the way back up

I did not know that

You had a ceremony

My feelings are hurt

My feelings are hurt

Because you're bitching at me

Instead of fixing

This migraine of mine

Seeps into my eye sockets

Makes it hard to see

The smoke curling up

From giant fires far away

Makes it hard to sleep

Every day I walk

Through a Korean Land mine

Unsure where to step

Unsure where to step

Trying to support all sides

But aren't both sides wrong?

Just to go to a

Rally with you would be good

To fight injustice

Let's fight injustice

By stepping back, lifting up

Those who need our help

When, where shall we meet?

Do let me know really soon

I do want to go

Shall we meet again?

So much of my heart hopes so

And yet there is pain

You tell them your life

I don't find out 'till later

I'm left in the dark.

I'm left in the dark

Wishing, waiting for quiet

The dark screams at me

I am blind to your

Knitted, hidden subtle talk

You talk in riddles.

You talk in riddles

Puzzling and intriguing but

Actual nonsense

I am really tired

Of just sitting on the couch

And not taking part

Not taking a part

In making the world better

But also, so tired

I see my dark soul

In the mirror - stares at me

With few illusions.

Few illusions left

Just disaster and nausea

Need a change to come

I would like to meet

The people you hang out with

Would be so awesome

Awesome: filled with awe

Overcome by beauty, grace

And magnificence

If you only knew

I wanted to marry you

Just not meant to be.

If you only knew

How many good things I wish

Would happen for you

I thought that we had

Something special between us

Just a masquerade.

Just a masquerade

Offering me the job and

Quick, now: change your mind!

I do wonder with

My Endometriosis:

Can I have a child?

Can I have a child?

Knowing what I know about

How hard the world is?

I keep wondering:

Will I find that special one?

Or end up alone.

Ending up alone

Somehow doesn't seem quite so

Terrifying, now

When I see others

Around me having children

I get really sad

I get really sad

Every time I think about

How lonely we are

You keep asking me:

Why don't I just kill myself?

Then you'd be happy.

You keep asking me

"Why don't I just kill myself?"

Because I love you

I would go to the

Ends of the earth if it meant

Me having a child

The end of the earth

Might be closer than we have

Ever imagined

In my quietest

Voice or my loudest whisper

I am never heard.

I am never heard

Even inside my own head

Too quiet? Or scared?

My voice remains as

Silent as a grain of sand:

Sahara Desert.

Sahara Desert:

Creeping larger faster than

Anticipated

I really want to

Be part of that other group

Having families

I think the others

Are just as scared and lonely

But not in photos

Your clothes and jewelry

Masked underneath vanity:

You have a black heart.

Black heart warrior

All battles bloody and lost

Where to go from here?

Vengeance doesn't bring

Peace to old bitter grudges

Put old ghosts to rest.

Chew bitter grudges

Like bitter ginger orange

Suck every last drop

If I killed myself

You would not shed any tears

You'd dance on my grave.

I do hope you danced

At least one time, please, just that

Even on my grave

In Conversation Vol. 4

What I really should

Do is some needle tatting

While watching TV

While watching TV

I keep being distracted

By the cutest dog

You're really lucky

You have her for company

I am all alone.

Company is nice

But they take up rental space

In my poor tired brain

I really do love

To do my needle tatting

Keeps my hands busy

Keep my hands busy

Lifting weights, throwing punches

Try to busy brain

What I really want:

What others have in their lives -

A special someone.

What I really want:

Meaningful work, exciting

Able to make change

I really can't wait

For August 22nd

Victoria trip

I really can't wait

For the world to both speed up

And slow down, at once

You only pretend

To be my very best friend

Just a bold faced lie.

I only pretend

To have my thoughts together

Really, all scrambled

I dream of great things

It doesn't matter what dream

Just that I have one.

I wonder about

How small my dreams have become:

To live, happily

I do not want to

Clean my room I do hate that

I would rather stitch

I do not want to

Do this stupid hard workout

It hurts me so much!

It is really hard

To be positive with such

Negativity

Negativity

Seems to fuel our twisted world

Breaking it further

My voice - a whale call:

Listen under the water -

It is loud and strong.

Under the water

I hear the faintest stirrings

Of beautiful song

Do you realize

What your words do to me

Angry, sad and mad

Angry, sad and mad

Too many feelings aching

Deep inside my heart

I like hanging out

With you in your apartment

It is relaxing.

It is relaxing

Making food for those I love

But not eating it

What if I told you

That I really do love you

How would you react?

How would you react

If I stamped my feet and screamed

Exactly like you?

I really want to

Go to that rally with you

So please do text me

I really want to

Explore the world as it is

Shake off all my fears

Your music helps me

To forget my living hell

Calms my inner soul.

Music takes my hand

Reminds me that it will be

Whatever it is

My fingers are the

Memory cards of every

Knitted stitch of yarn.

Knitted stitches fall

Tug apart and weave themselves

Into new clothing

I keep wondering:

What is it really like to

Have a child in me?

I keep wondering:

How to best support my child

Should I be blessed

When my father died

I cried bitter tears of grief

I was all alone.

I was all alone

The darkness creeping, cat-like

But the sun came up

I do think about

Me having my own children

All consuming thoughts

All consuming faith

That everything will turn out

As it is meant to

To have a special

Someone in my life to be

My own family.

My own family

Drives me bonkers most times but

I still love them all

A set of in-laws

I could spend lots of time with

People to love me.

People to love me

Support, care, and lift me up

Isn't that the dream?

I love being kissed

Two people in an embrace

Sharing their feelings

Sharing my feelings

Seems to rebound badly

Should keep them locked tight

Just to hear those words:
"I love you" from him to me
Precious drops of gold.

Precious drops of gold
Sunny haired children, flowers
Long sunny filled days

There are days that I

Keep on wondering if I

Really do have friends

There are days that I

Wonder what my life comes to

Balanced at the end

My family anchor

Is filled with false honey smiles

Poisonous venom.

Poisonous venom

Seeps through my best intentions

Ruins everything

Maybe I don't dance

But if it were you and me

Then perhaps I would

Maybe I don't learn

But I'd rather lose it all

Than refuse to trust

We walk amongst the

Dead/unseen souls who have walked

The Earth before us.

Unseen souls fly past

Desperately wishing to

Save us from ourselves

When I see myself

In the mirror I only

See an ugly soul

When I see myself

I try to reconcile that

Somehow, I am loved

There is a saying

That Jesus didn't tap 'cause

He loved to play jazz.

Jesus would have been

An excellent jazz player

He knew his own heart

It would be awesome

To sing in a choir but

Where can I do that?

To sing in a choir

Is to lift my heart and soul

Offer all to God

Knitting feeds my soul

It makes my inner self whole

Lack of it: a loss.

Lack of love: a loss

Unbearable and cruel

Yet, I soldier on

I really do want

A father in my life to

Tell him my secrets

Telling my secrets?

Oh no, couldn't possibly

You'd stop loving me

The words that you use:

A Minotaur's Labyrinth -

Nothing: But a maze.

My mind is a maze

Twists and turns and dead ends but

Somewhere there's a map

I really wish that

My father had not left me

Angry and depressed

Angry and depressed:

Name of my biography

But did I use it?

You said that I have

Alienated my kin

Just a bold faced lie.

You said that I have

Greater challenges in store

I wish I didn't

If I only had

A sibling I could talk to

Someone to confide

If I only had

Enough backbone to tell you

How I really feel

Why do you insist

On spitting out your venom

To hurt my feelings?

My feelings aren't hurt

There are too few of them left

For you to hurt me

I'm really hungry

I really do want to eat

Supper right away

I'm really hungry

Want a plate full of Justice

With a cup of love

Movie violence

I do not like all of that

It makes me feel sick

I do not like it

This violent discussion

About who is right

An argument should be

A bounce house where grudges will

Not stick to the wall.

An argument's never

What I expect it will be -

Always loud and worse

I really miss my

Cats Phantom, Opera, Spot

I love them a lot

I really missed out

On the opportunity

To adopt a dog

When both of us kiss

It is just the two of us

Lips melting away

Just the two of us

Trying to make sense of all

In a crazy world

An opportunity

Comes: Everything is today

Nothing - tomorrow.

An opportunity

Or perhaps a chore, I think

I'll wait to find out

You are Bear to me

You calm me when I'm upset

Warm, soothing blanket.

I'm a bear today

Grumpy, take up too much space

Eating everything

When you told me that

On the phone after Christmas

I still remember

I still remember

The magic of Christmas Day

Woke up to wonder

The grass is really

Not greener on this side of

This fence: Trick of light.

Tricking of the light

The days get shorter but the

Nights stay long and cold

The way it should be:

Leave other people alone

Mind your own business.

Mind your own business

But with specific kindness

Go do something good

I really wonder:

If one day you'll say to me

The words: "I love you".

The words "I love you"

Are said both too frequently

Also not enough

www.ingramcontent.com/pod-product-compliance
Lightning Source LLC
Chambersburg PA
CBHW070306120526
44590CB00017B/2581